GOD'S LITTLE INSTRUCTION BOOK

FOR THE CLASS OF 2009

GOD'S LITTLE INSTRUCTION BOOK

INSTRUCTION BOOK

FOR THE CLASS OF 2009

David C Cook®

transforming lives together

GOD'S LITTLE INSTRUCTION BOOK FOR THE CLASS OF 2009

David C. Cook
4050 Lee Vance View
Colorado Springs, CO 80918 U.S.A.

David C. Cook Distribution Canada
55 Woodslee Avenue, Paris, Ontario, Canada N3L 3E5

David C. Cook U.K., Kingsway Communications
Eastbourne, East Sussex BN23 6NT, England

ISBN 978-1-4347-6598-7

The Team: Ingrid Beck, Melanie Larson, Amy Kiechlin, Jaci Schneider, and Caitlyn York
Interior Design: Karen Athen
Cover Design: studiogearbox.com
Cover Photo: iStockphoto

Printed in Canada
First Edition 2009

1 2 3 4 5 6 7 8 9 10

010509

Congratulations! As a member of the Class of 2009, you have the privilege and responsibility of being part of the most important group of people on earth—those who will be setting the pace, establishing the values, and initiating the changes for a world that suddenly finds itself face-to-face with the future.

Like every generation that has come before, you will encounter enormous challenges as well as amazing opportunities. And you are bound to find that you will be confronted with difficult questions and complex issues for which there are no precedents. You will truly be going where no one has gone before—except God! How will you find the answers you need?

In *God's Little Instruction Book for the Class of 2009*, we at David C. Cook offer you God's timeless wisdom taken from the one book that will never be obsolete—the Bible. We hope the truths presented in these pages will serve as cherished resources for you as you launch out into the depths of human possibility and potential.

FOR THE CLASS OF 2009

Not fare well, but fare forward, voyagers.
—T. S. Eliot

I am with you and will watch over you wherever you go.

Genesis 28:15

FOR THE CLASS OF 2009

Some people succeed because they are destined to, but most people succeed because they are determined to.
—HENRY WADSWORTH LONGFELLOW

Having done all, to stand .... Stand therefore.

Ephesians 6:13–14 KJV

FOR THE CLASS OF 2009

The journey of a thousand miles
begins with one step.
—Lao-tzu

**For God did not give us a spirit of
timidity, but a spirit of power, of love
and of self-discipline.**

2 Timothy 1:7

FOR THE CLASS OF 2009

You are only what you are
when no one is looking.
—Robert C. Edwards

**Not with eyeservice, as menpleasers;
but as the servants of Christ, doing the
will of God from the heart.**

Ephesians 6:6 KJV

God is the God of promise. He keeps His word, even when that seems impossible, even when the circumstances seem to point to the opposite.

—COLIN URQUHART

What I have said, that will I bring about; what I have planned, that will I do.

Isaiah 46:11

FOR THE CLASS OF 2009

Laughter gives us distance. It allows us to step back
from an event, deal with it, and then move on.
—BOB NEWHART

**For our light affliction, which is but for
a moment, is working for us a far more
exceeding and eternal weight of glory.**

2 Corinthians 4:17 NKJV

FOR THE CLASS OF 2009

Wise men talk because they have something to say; fools, because they have to say something.
—PLATO

The mouth of the righteous man utters wisdom, and his tongue speaks what is just.

Psalm 37:30

FOR THE CLASS OF 2009

Who finds a faithful friend finds a treasure.
—Jewish Saying

If one falls down, his friend can help him up. But pity the man who falls and has no one to help him up!

Ecclesiastes 4:10

Conquer yourself rather than the world.
—DESCARTES

Similarly, encourage the young men to be self-controlled.

Titus 2:6

FOR THE CLASS OF 2009

We must accept finite disappointment,
but never lose infinite hope.
—MARTIN LUTHER KING JR.

Though he slay me, yet will I hope in him.

Job 13:15

The only way to learn strong faith
is to endure great trials.
—GEORGE MÜLLER

My dear brothers, stand firm. Let nothing move you. Always give yourselves fully to the work of the Lord, because you know that your labor in the Lord is not in vain.

1 Corinthians 15:58

FOR THE CLASS OF 2009

Speak when you are angry—and you'll
make the best speech you'll ever regret.
—LAURENCE J. PETER

**Watch your words and hold your
tongue; you'll save yourself a lot of
grief.**

Proverbs 21:23 MSG

Wisdom is not a product of schooling
but of the lifelong attempt to acquire it.
—ALBERT EINSTEIN

**Wisdom and truth will enter the very
center of your being, filling your life
with joy.**

Proverbs 2:10 TLB

FOR THE CLASS OF 2009

We are all faced with a series of
great opportunities brilliantly
disguised as impossible situations.
—CHARLES R. SWINDOLL

**Fight the good fight of the faith. Take
hold of the eternal life to which you
were called when you made your good
confession in the presence of many
witnesses.**

1 Timothy 6:12

FOR THE CLASS OF 2009

Give your problems to God; He
will be up all night anyway.
—MARY CROWLEY

**And even the very hairs of your
head are all numbered. So don't be
afraid; you are worth more than many
sparrows.**

Matthew 10:30–31

FOR THE CLASS OF 2009

When the character of a man is not
clear to you, look at his friends.
—JAPANESE PROVERB

**A righteous man is cautious in
friendship.**

Proverbs 12:26

Every tomorrow has two handles. We can take hold of it by the handle of anxiety, or by the handle of faith.
—HENRY WARD BEECHER

Cast all your anxiety on him because he cares for you.

1 Peter 5:7

FOR THE CLASS OF 2009

We need to pay more attention to how we treat people than to how they treat us.
—JOYCE MEYERS

Love others as well as you love yourself.

Mark 12:31 MSG

Don't fear change—embrace it.
—ANTHONY J. D'ANGELO

I am leaving you with a gift—peace of mind and heart! And the peace I give isn't fragile like the peace the world gives. So don't be troubled or afraid.

John 14:27 TLB

FOR THE CLASS OF 2009

All works of love are works of peace.
—MOTHER TERESA

I have told you these things, so that in me you may have peace. In this world you will have trouble. But take heart! I have overcome the world.

John 16:33

Believe in yourself! Have faith in your abilities!
Without a humble but reasonable confidence in your
own powers you cannot be successful or happy.
—NORMAN VINCENT PEALE

**There's nothing better than being wise,
knowing how to interpret the meaning
of life. Wisdom puts light in the eyes,
and gives gentleness to words and
manners.**

Ecclesiastes 8:1 MSG

FOR THE CLASS OF 2009

We live in deeds, not years; in
thoughts, not breaths. We should
count time by heartthrobs. He
most lives who thinks most—feels
the noblest—acts the best.
—P. J. BAILEY

"For in him we live and move and have
our being." As some of your own poets
have said, "We are his offspring."

Acts 17:28

FOR THE CLASS OF 2009

Where I found truth, there found I
my God, who is the truth itself.
—St. Augustine

**Seek first his kingdom and his
righteousness, and all these things will
be given to you as well.**

Matthew 6:33

FOR THE CLASS OF 2009

Every calling is great when greatly pursued.
—JULIA CARNEY

I press toward the mark for the prize of the high calling of God in Christ Jesus.

Philippians 3:14 KJV

Willpower does not change men. Time
does not change men. Christ does.
—HENRY DRUMMOND

Now to him who is able to do
immeasurably more than all we ask or
imagine, according to his power that is
at work within us.

Ephesians 3:20

FOR THE CLASS OF 2009

The most important single ingredient
in the formula of success is knowing
how to get along with people.
—THEODORE ROOSEVELT

**See that no one pays back evil for evil,
but always try to do good to each other
and to everyone else.**

1 Thessalonians 5:15 TLB

FOR THE CLASS OF 2009

The only way to discover the limits
of the possible is to go beyond
them into the impossible.
—ARTHUR C. CLARKE

**Jesus said to him, "If you can believe,
all things are possible to him who
believes."**

Mark 9:23 NKJV

FOR THE CLASS OF 2009

Contentment is directly proportionate
to the measure you give of yourself.
—UNKNOWN

**Therefore, as we have opportunity, let
us do good to all people.**

Galatians 6:10

Effort only fully releases its reward
after a person refuses to quit.
—NAPOLEON HILL

Don't quit in hard times; pray all the harder.

Romans 12:12 MSG

FOR THE CLASS OF 2009

People may doubt what you say, but
they will believe what you do.
—JAMES THURBER

**My little children, let us not love in
word, neither in tongue; but in deed
and in truth.**

1 John 3:18 KJV

FOR THE CLASS OF 2009

Death is more universal than life;
everyone dies; not everyone lives.
—A. Sachs

**I have come that they may have life,
and have it to the full.**

John 10:10

FOR THE CLASS OF 2009

When we long for life without difficulties, remind us that oaks grow strong in contrary winds and diamonds are made under pressure.
—PETER MARSHALL

Perseverance must finish its work so that you may be mature and complete, not lacking anything.

James 1:4

Be courteous to all, but intimate with few, and let those few be well tried before you give them your confidence.
—GEORGE WASHINGTON

He who walks with wise men will be wise.

Proverbs 13:20 NKJV

FOR THE CLASS OF 2009

God will not demand more from you than
you can do. Whatever God asks of you,
He will give you the strength to do.
—ERWIN W. LUTZER

**So now, go. I am sending you to
Pharaoh to bring my people the
Israelites out of Egypt.**

Exodus 3:10

We can believe what we choose. We are answerable for what we choose to believe.
—JOHN HENRY NEWMAN

But without faith it is impossible to please Him, for he who comes to God must believe that He is, and that He is a rewarder of those who diligently seek Him.

Hebrews 11:6 NKJV

FOR THE CLASS OF 2009

Do not follow where the path may lead. Go instead where there is no path and leave a trail.
—St. Thomas Acquinas

Your ears shall hear a word behind you, saying, "This is the way, walk in it."

Isaiah 30:21 NKJV

FOR THE CLASS OF 2009

Real knowledge is to know the
extent of one's ignorance.
—CONFUCIUS

**But ye seek first the kingdom of God,
and his righteousness; and all these
things shall be added unto you.**

Matthew 6:33 KJV

FOR THE CLASS OF 2009

The golden rule for understanding in spiritual matters is not intellect, but obedience.
—OSWALD CHAMBERS

Here's how we can be sure that we know God in the right way: Keep his commandments.

1 John 2:3 MSG

When you come to the end of your
rope ... tie a knot and hang on.
—FRANKLIN D. ROOSEVELT

**Who of you by worrying can add a
single hour to his life?**

Matthew 6:27

FOR THE CLASS OF 2009

What the caterpillar calls the end of the
world the master calls a butterfly.
—RICHARD BACH

**And we, who with unveiled faces all
reflect the Lord's glory, are being
transformed into his likeness with
ever-increasing glory.**

2 Corinthians 3:18

A ship in harbor is safe, but that is
not what ships are built for.
—WILLIAM SHEDD

**You are the world's light—a city on a
hill, glowing in the night for all to see.
Don't hide your light!**

Matthew 5:14-15 TLB

The capacity to care is the thing which gives life its deepest significance.
—PABLO CASALS

Carry each other's burdens, and in this way you will fulfill the law of Christ.

Galatians 6:2

FOR THE CLASS OF 2009

I try to avoid looking forward or backward,
and try to keep looking upward.
—CHARLOTTE BRONTË

**I have set the Lord always before me.
Because he is at my right hand, I will
not be shaken.**

Psalm 16:8

FOR THE CLASS OF 2009

God does not love us because we are valuable.
We are valuable because God loves us.
—ARCHBISHOP FULTON J. SHEEN

**The LORD delights in those who
fear him, who put their hope in his
unfailing love.**

Psalm 147:11

FOR THE CLASS OF 2009

We make a living by what we get—
we make a life by what we give.
—Arnold Glasgow

It is more blessed to give than to receive.

Acts 20:35 NASB

You can tell the character of every man
when you see how he receives praise.
—SENECA

**God resists the proud, but gives grace
to the humble.**

James 4:6 NKJV

FOR THE CLASS OF 2009

Every action of our lives touches on some chord that will vibrate in eternity.
—EDWIN HUBBEL CHAPIN

In the same way, let your light shine before men, that they may see your good deeds and praise your Father in heaven.

Matthew 5:16

FOR THE CLASS OF 2009

Life can only be understood backwards;
but it must be lived forwards.
—SØREN KIERKEGAARD

This is what the LORD says—your Redeemer, the Holy One of Israel: "I am the LORD your God, who teaches you what is best for you, who directs you in the way you should go."

Isaiah 48:17

FOR THE CLASS OF 2009

It is amidst great perils that we see brave hearts.
—JEAN FRANCOIS REGNARD

**I will not fear the tens of thousands
drawn up against me on every side.**

Psalm 3:6

FOR THE CLASS OF 2009

Don't allow the future to scare you.
—TENNESSEE WILLIAMS

Whoever trusts in the LORD is kept safe.

Proverbs 29:25

How wonderful it is that nobody need wait a single moment before starting to improve the world.
—ANNE FRANK

As we have opportunity, let us do good to all people.

Galatians 6:10

FOR THE CLASS OF 2009

Obedience to the call of Christ nearly always costs everything to two people: the one who is called, and the one who loves that one.
—OSWALD CHAMBERS

If you will indeed obey My voice and keep My covenant, then you shall be a special treasure to Me above all people; for all the earth is Mine.

Exodus 19:5 NKJV

FOR THE CLASS OF 2009

Most of the things worth doing in the world had
been declared impossible before they were done.
—LOUIS D. BRANDEIS

With God all things are possible.

Matthew 19:26 KJV

Great men are little men expanded; great
lives are ordinary lives intensified.
—WILFRED A. PETERSON

**Those who have served well gain an
excellent standing and great assurance
in their faith in Christ Jesus.**

1 Timothy 3:13

FOR THE CLASS OF 2009

Character is doing the right thing when nobody's looking. There are too many people who think that the only thing that's right is to get by, and the only thing that's wrong is to get caught.
—J. C. Watts

There is a way that seems right to a man, but in the end it leads to death.

Proverbs 14:12

FOR THE CLASS OF 2009

Give light, and the darkness will disappear of itself.
—DESIDERIUS ERASMUS

God saw that the light was good, and He separated the light from the darkness.

Genesis 1:4

FOR THE CLASS OF 2009

Theology is just what you really think
about God, and if you're going to do that,
you'd better use your mind and not just let
it be a receptacle, a catch-all for whatever
beliefs happen to be passing by.
—DALLAS WILLARD

**For the word of God is living and active.
Sharper than any double-edged sword, it
penetrates even to dividing soul and spirit,
joints and marrow; it judges the thoughts
and attitudes of the heart.**

Hebrews 4:12

FOR THE CLASS OF 2009

We are made strong by the difficulties
we face, not by those we evade.
—UNKNOWN

**In all these things we are more than
conquerors through him who loved us.**

Romans 8:37

Who lives in fear will never be a free man.
—HORACE

The LORD is with me; I will not be afraid.

Psalm 118:6

FOR THE CLASS OF 2009

God made the world round, so we would never be able to see too far down the road.
—ISAK DINESEN

"For I know the plans I have for you," declares the Lord, "plans to prosper you and not to harm you, plans to give you hope and a future."

Jeremiah 29:11

FOR THE CLASS OF 2009

The difference between ordinary and
extraordinary is that little extra effort.
—HOMER

**Whatsoever thy hand findeth to do, do
it with thy might.**

Ecclesiastes 9:10 KJV

FOR THE CLASS OF 2009

Cast your cares on God; that anchor holds.
—ALFRED LORD TENNYSON

I will say of the Lord, "He is my refuge and my fortress, my God, in whom I trust."

Psalm 91:2

To speak painful truth through loving
words, that is friendship.
—HENRY WARD BEECHER

Faithful are the wounds of a friend.

Proverbs 27:6 NKJV

FOR THE CLASS OF 2009

To love what you do and feel that it matters—how could anything be more fun?
—KATHERINE GRAHAM

For my heart rejoiced in all my labour.

Ecclesiastes 2:10 KJV

FOR THE CLASS OF 2009

God's help is nearer than the door.
—Irish Proverb

I am with you and will watch over you wherever you go.

Genesis 28:15

FOR THE CLASS OF 2009

Do not borrow trouble by dreading
tomorrow. It is the dark menace of the
future that makes cowards of us all.
—DOROTHY DIX

**For he will command his angels
concerning you to guard you in all
your ways.**

Psalm 91:11

FOR THE CLASS OF 2009

Thoughts lead on to purposes; purposes go forth
in action; actions form habits; habits decide
character; and character fixes our destiny.
—TYRON EDWARDS

**The purposes of a man's heart are deep
waters, but a man of understanding
draws them out.**

Proverbs 20:5

Have courage for the great sorrows of life and patience for the small ones; and when you have laboriously accomplished your daily task, go to sleep in peace. God is awake.
—Victor Hugo

He will not let your foot slip—he who watches over you will not slumber.

Psalm 121:3

FOR THE CLASS OF 2009

God dwells in eternity, but time dwells
in God. He has already lived all our
tomorrows as He has lived all our yesterdays.
—A. W. TOZER

**Surely I am with you always, to the
very end of the age.**

Matthew 28:20

FOR THE CLASS OF 2009

Courage is the power to let go of the familiar.
—MARY BRYANT

**The Lord is the stronghold of my life—
of whom shall I be afraid?**

Psalm 27:1

FOR THE CLASS OF 2009

Let your words be the genuine picture of your heart.
—JOHN WESLEY

My mouth shall speak wisdom, and the meditation of my heart shall give understanding.

Psalm 49:3 NKJV

FOR THE CLASS OF 2009

Let there be kindness in your face, in your eyes, in your smile, in the warmth of your greeting.... Don't only give your care, but give your heart as well.
—MOTHER TERESA

Do not forget to do good and to share with others, for with such sacrifices God is pleased.

Hebrews 13:16

Stand upright, speak thy thoughts,
declare the truth thou hast, that
all may share; Be bold, proclaim it
everywhere: They only live who dare.
—LEWIS MORRIS

Speaking the truth in love, we will in all things grow up into him who is the Head, that is, Christ.

Ephesians 4:15

FOR THE CLASS OF 2009

Money is a good servant but a bad master.
—SIR FRANCIS BACON

The rich rule over the poor, and the borrower is servant to the lender.

Proverbs 22:7

FOR THE CLASS OF 2009

Every man is a missionary, now and forever, for good or for evil, whether he intends or designs it or not.
—THOMAS CHALMERS

I have set before you life and death, blessing and cursing; therefore choose life, that both you and your descendants may live.

Deuteronomy 30:19 NKJV

FOR THE CLASS OF 2009

It often happens that those of whom we speak least on earth are best known in heaven.
—Nicholas Caussin

You are a chosen people, a royal priesthood, a holy nation, a people belonging to God, that you may declare the praises of him who called you out of darkness into his wonderful light.

1 Peter 2:9

FOR THE CLASS OF 2009

Identify your highest skill and devote
your time to performing it.
—Johann Wolfgang von Goethe

**Give diligence to make your calling
and election sure: for if ye do these
things, ye shall never fall.**

2 Peter 1:10 KJV

FOR THE CLASS OF 2009

Missions is less about the transportation of God from one place to another and more about the identification of a God who is already there.
—ROB BELL

And whatever you do, whether in word or deed, do it all in the name of the Lord Jesus, giving thanks to God the Father through him.

Colossians 3:17

FOR THE CLASS OF 2009

Snuggle in God's arms. When you are hurting, when you feel lonely, left out, let Him cradle you, comfort you, reassure you of His all-sufficient power and love.
—KAY ARTHUR

Staying right at the center of God's love, keeping your arms open and outstretched, ready for the mercy of our Master, Jesus Christ. This is the unending life, the real life!

Jude 1:21 MSG

FOR THE CLASS OF 2009

I am an old man and have known a great many troubles, but most of them never happened.
—MARK TWAIN

I will lie down and sleep in peace, for you alone, O LORD, make me dwell in safety.

Psalm 4:8

FOR THE CLASS OF 2009

God never put anyone in a place too small to grow in.
—HENRIETTA CORNELIA MEARS

Give thanks in all circumstances, for this is God's will for you in Christ Jesus.

1 Thessalonians 5:18

FOR THE CLASS OF 2009

Smart is believing half of what you hear;
brilliant is knowing which half to believe.
—SERGE BIRBRAIR

**For wisdom and truth will enter the
very center of your being, filling your
life with joy.**

Proverbs 2:10 TLB

FOR THE CLASS OF 2009

Faith is not belief without proof,
but trust without reservations.
—ELTON TRUEBLOOD

As for God, His way is perfect; the
word of the Lord is proven; He is a
shield to all who trust in Him.

Psalm 18:30 NKJV

FOR THE CLASS OF 2009

The most revolutionary statement in
history is "Love Thy Enemy."
—ELDRIDGE CLEAVER

**This is love: not that we loved God,
but that he loved us and sent his Son
as an atoning sacrifice for our sins.**

1 John 4:10

FOR THE CLASS OF 2009

Everything that is done in the
world is done by hope.
—Martin Luther

**Find rest, O my soul, in God alone; my
hope comes from him.**

Psalm 62:5

FOR THE CLASS OF 2009

Thanksgiving is the language of heaven,
and we had better start to learn it if we
are not to be mere dumb aliens there.
—A. J. Gossip

**For every creature of God is good, and
nothing is to be refused if it is received
with thanksgiving.**

1 Timothy 4:4 NKJV

FOR THE CLASS OF 2009

Within your heart keep one still,
secret spot where dreams may go and,
sheltered so, may thrive and grow.
—LOUISE DRISCOLL

**Above all else, guard your heart, for it
is the wellspring of life.**

Proverbs 4:23

FOR THE CLASS OF 2009

The best bridge between hope and despair
is often a good night's sleep.
—HERACLEITUS

**It is vain for you to rise up early, to sit
up late, to eat the bread of sorrows: for
so he giveth his beloved sleep.**

Psalm 127:2 KJV

We get one story, you and I, and one story alone.
God has established the elements, the setting, and
the climax and the resolution. It would be
a crime not to venture out, wouldn't it?
—Donald Miller

**Whether you turn to the right or to
the left, your ears will hear a voice
behind you, saying, "This is the way;
walk in it."**

Isaiah 30:21

FOR THE CLASS OF 2009

God is not a deceiver, that He should offer
to support us, and then, when we lean
upon Him, should slip away from us.
—ST. AUGUSTINE

**Guard my life, for I am devoted to you.
You are my God; save your servant
who trusts in you.**

Psalm 86:2

Nothing is worth more than this day.
—JOHANN WOLFGANG VON GOETHE

The day is yours, and yours also the night; you established the sun and moon.

Psalm 74:16

FOR THE CLASS OF 2009

Without prayer, we return to our own
ability rather than to God.
—BETH MOORE

**I am glad to boast about how
weak I am; I am glad to be a living
demonstration of Christ's power,
instead of showing off my own power
and abilities.**

2 Corinthians 12:9 TLB

God does not give us everything we want, but He does fulfill His promises … leading us along the best and straightest paths to Himself.

—DIETRICH BONHOEFFER

In everything you do, put God first, and he will direct you and crown your efforts with success.

Proverbs 3:6 TLB

FOR THE CLASS OF 2009

Pray for just enough illumination for the next step, and then the courage to take it.
—DAVID CROWDER

Be joyful in hope, patient in affliction, faithful in prayer.

Romans 12:12

Humor is to life what shock
absorbers are to automobiles.
—JONATHAN SWIFT

**A merry heart doeth good like a
medicine: but a broken spirit drieth the
bones.**

Proverbs 17:22 KJV

FOR THE CLASS OF 2009

Never fear shadows. They simply mean there's light shining somewhere nearby.
—RUTH E. RENKEL

Yea, though I walk through the valley of the shadow of death, I will fear no evil; for You are with me; Your rod and Your staff, they comfort me.

Psalm 23:4 NKJV

Few things are impossible to diligence
and skill. Great works are performed,
not by strength, but perseverance.
—SAMUEL JOHNSON

**We want each of you to show this same
diligence to the very end, in order to
make your hope sure.**

Hebrews 6:11

FOR THE CLASS OF 2009

My faith isn't in the idea that I'm more moral than anybody else. My faith is in the idea that God and His love are greater than whatever sins any of us commit.
—RICH MULLINS

I sought the LORD, and he answered me; he delivered me from all my fears.

Psalm 34:4

Fear defeats more people than any
other one thing in the world.
—RALPH WALDO EMERSON

Perfect love drives out fear.

1 John 4:18

FOR THE CLASS OF 2009

I think the one lesson I have learned is that there is no substitute for paying attention.
—DIANE SAWYER

Therefore we ought to give the more earnest heed to the things which we have heard, lest at any time we should let them slip.

Hebrews 2:1 KJV

FOR THE CLASS OF 2009

Take time to deliberate; but when the time for action arrives, stop thinking and go on.
—ANDREW JACKSON

Rise up; this matter is in your hands. We will support you, so take courage and do it.

Ezra 10:4

FOR THE CLASS OF 2009

Any definition of a successful life
must include serving others.
—George H. W. Bush

**He who is greatest among you shall be
your servant.**

Matthew 23:11 NKJV

Happiness depends on what happens; joy does not.
—Oswald Chambers

You have made known to me the path of life; you will fill me with joy in your presence, with eternal pleasures at your right hand.

Psalm 16:11

FOR THE CLASS OF 2009

Act boldly and unseen forces will come to your aid.
—DOROTHEA BRANDE

We have the Lord our God to fight our battles for us!

2 Chronicles 32:8 TLB

FOR THE CLASS OF 2009

The future belongs to those who believe
in the beauty of their dreams.
—ELEANOR ROOSEVELT

Anything is possible if you have faith.

Mark 9:23 TLB

FOR THE CLASS OF 2009

Pray often, for prayer is a shield to the soul,
a sacrifice to God, and a scourge for Satan.
—JOHN BUNYAN

**The prayer of a righteous man is
powerful and effective.**

James 5:16

FOR THE CLASS OF 2009

The essence of temptation is the invitation
to live independently of God.

—NEIL ANDERSON

**I am the vine; you are the branches.
If a man remains in me and I in him,
he will bear much fruit; apart from me
you can do nothing.**

John 15:5

FOR THE CLASS OF 2009

Shoot for the moon. Even if you miss,
you will land among the stars.
—LES BROWN

Aim for perfection.

2 Corinthians 13:11

Learn the luxury of doing good.
—Oliver Goldsmith

Do not withhold good from those who deserve it, when it is in your power to act.

Proverbs 3:27

FOR THE CLASS OF 2009

I am convinced that faith sometimes means knowing God can, whether or not He does.
—BETH MOORE

If we are thrown into the blazing furnace, the God we serve is able to save us from it.... But even if he does not, we want you to know, O king, that we will not serve your gods.

Daniel 3:17-18

FOR THE CLASS OF 2009

Truth, like surgery, may hurt but it cures.
—HAN SUYIN

Speaking the truth in love, we will in all things grow up into him who is the Head, that is, Christ.

Ephesians 4:15

FOR THE CLASS OF 2009

Living in the moment brings you a sense of reverence for all of life's blessings.
—OPRAH WINFREY

So don't be anxious about tomorrow. God will take care of your tomorrow too. Live one day at a time.

Matthew 6:34 TLB

The secret of success is to do the
common things uncommonly well.
—JOHN D. ROCKEFELLER JR.

**Seest thou a man diligent in his
business? He shall stand before kings;
he shall not stand before mean men.**

Proverbs 22:29 KJV

FOR THE CLASS OF 2009

No sacrifice can be too great to make for
Him who gave His life for me.
—CHARLES STUDD

**Christ's love compels us, because we
are convinced that one died for all.**

2 Corinthians 5:14

If peace be in the heart, the wildest
winter storm is full of solemn beauty.
—C. F. RICHARDSON

**And the peace of God, which
transcends all understanding, will
guard your hearts and your minds in
Christ Jesus.**

Philippians 4:7

FOR THE CLASS OF 2009

Love is pressing around us on all sides like air. Cease to resist it and instantly love takes possession.

—AMY CARMICHAEL

This is love: not that we loved God, but that he loved us and sent his Son as an atoning sacrifice for our sins.

1 John 4:10

FOR THE CLASS OF 2009

The Scriptures were not given to increase
our knowledge but to change our lives.
—D. L. MOODY

**Show me your ways, O LORD, teach me
your paths.**

Psalm 25:4

What we are is God's gift to us. What
we become is our gift to God.
—ELEANOR POWELL

**Every good and perfect gift is from
above, coming down from the Father of
the heavenly lights.**

James 1:17

FOR THE CLASS OF 2009

Believe in something larger than yourself.
—BARBARA BUSH

Now faith is the substance of things hoped for, the evidence of things not seen.

Hebrews 11:1 NKJV

Call on God, but row away from the rocks.
—HUNTER S. THOMPSON

**Wisdom and good judgment
live together, for wisdom knows
where to discover knowledge and
understanding.**

Proverbs 8:12 TLB

FOR THE CLASS OF 2009

You can lead a boy to college, but
you cannot make him think.
—KIN HUBBARD

**It is senseless to pay tuition to educate
a rebel who has no heart for truth.**

Proverbs 17:16 TLB

FOR THE CLASS OF 2009

Though our feelings come and go,
God's love for us does not.
—C. S. Lewis

**Great is his faithfulness; his
lovingkindness begins afresh each day.**

Lamentations 3:23 TLB

FOR THE CLASS OF 2009

Success consists of getting up just
one more time than you fall.
—Oliver Goldsmith

**I can do everything through him who
gives me strength.**

Philippians 4:13

FOR THE CLASS OF 2009

The best things are nearest:
breath in your nostrils, light
in your eyes, flowers at your
feet, duties at your hand, the
path of God just before you.
—ROBERT LOUIS STEVENSON

Give thanks to the LORD, for he is good; his love endures forever.

1 Chronicles 16:34

FOR THE CLASS OF 2009

Sainthood lies in the habit of referring
the smallest actions to God.
—C. S. Lewis

**Praise Him for His mighty acts;
praise Him according to His excellent
greatness!**

Psalm 150:2 NKJV

FOR THE CLASS OF 2009

The stars are constantly shining, but often we
do not see them until the dark hours.
—EARL RINEY

**My help comes from the LORD, the
Maker of heaven and earth.**

Psalm 121:2

Opportunities are seldom labeled.
—JOHN A. SHEDD

Seek, and ye shall find; knock, and it shall be opened unto you.

Matthew 7:7 KJV

FOR THE CLASS OF 2009

I have decided to stick with love. Hate is too great a burden to bear.
—MARTIN LUTHER KING JR.

Do everything in love.

1 Corinthians 16:14

At the height of laughter, the universe is flung into a kaleidoscope of new possibilities.
—JEAN HOUSTON

He will yet fill your mouth with laughter and your lips with shouts of joy.

Job 8:21

FOR THE CLASS OF 2009

Your worst days are never so bad
that you are beyond the reach of
God's grace. And your best days
are never so good that you are
beyond the need of God's grace.
—JERRY BRIDGES

**God can pour on the blessings in
astonishing ways so that you're ready
for anything and everything, more than
just ready to do what needs to be done.**

2 Corinthians 9:8 MSG

FOR THE CLASS OF 2009

Learn from yesterday; live for
today; hope for tomorrow.
—ALBERT EINSTEIN

**We have this hope as an anchor for the
soul, firm and secure.**

Hebrews 6:19

FOR THE CLASS OF 2009

Blessed is the man who finds out which way God is moving and then gets going in the same direction.
—UNKNOWN

Whether you turn to the right or to the left, your ears will hear a voice behind you, saying, "This is the way; walk in it."

Isaiah 30:21

FOR THE CLASS OF 2009

Four things for success: Work and
pray, think and believe.
—NORMAN VINCENT PEALE

**But as for you, be strong and do
not give up, for your work will be
rewarded.**

2 Chronicles 15:7

FOR THE CLASS OF 2009

Beware that you do not lose the substance
by grasping at the shadow.
—AESOP

Give your servant a discerning heart.

1 Kings 3:9

Debt is the worst poverty.
—THOMAS FULLER

The borrower is servant to the lender.

Proverbs 22:7

FOR THE CLASS OF 2009

Never be afraid to trust an unknown
future to a known God.
—CORRIE TEN BOOM

**I will turn the darkness into light
before them and make the rough places
smooth.**

Isaiah 42:16

FOR THE CLASS OF 2009

The future lies before you, like paths of pure white snow. Be careful how you tread it, for every step will show.

—UNKNOWN

In everything you do, put God first, and he will direct you and crown your efforts with success.

Proverbs 3:6 TLB

FOR THE CLASS OF 2009

Where fear is present, wisdom cannot be.
—Lucius C. Lactantius

The Lord is my light and my salvation—whom shall I fear?

Psalm 27:1

FOR THE CLASS OF 2009

Maturity doesn't come with age; it comes
with acceptance of responsibility.
—ALEXANDER MACLAREN

**When I was a child, I spake as a child,
I understood as a child, I thought as a
child; but when I became a man, I put
away childish things.**

1 Corinthians 13:11 KJV

FOR THE CLASS OF 2009

When I despair, I remember that all through history, the way of truth and love has always won.
—MAHATMA GANDHI

The Lord knows how to rescue godly men from trials.

2 Peter 2:9

A Christian is someone who shares the
sufferings of God in the world.
—DIETRICH BONHOEFFER

**Consider it pure joy, my brothers,
whenever you face trials of many
kinds, because you know that
the testing of your faith develops
perseverance.**

James 1:2-3

FOR THE CLASS OF 2009

Always seek peace between your heart and
God, but in this world, always be careful
to remain ever-restless, never satisfied, and
always abounding in the work of the Lord.
—JIM ELLIOT

**In everything set them an example by
doing what is good.**

Titus 2:7

FOR THE CLASS OF 2009

Learn by experience—preferably other people's.
—F. B. MEYER

All these things happened to them as examples—as object lessons to us—to warn us against doing the same things.

1 Corinthians 10:11 TLB

FOR THE CLASS OF 2009

Avoiding danger is no safer in the long run than outright exposure. Life is either a daring adventure, or nothing.
—HELEN KELLER

Alive, I'm Christ's messenger; dead, I'm his bounty. Life versus even more life! I can't lose.

Philippians 1:21 MSG

The goal of life is to find out God's will and to do it.
—MARIA VON TRAPP

**Just tell me what to do and I will
do it, Lord. As long as I live I'll
wholeheartedly obey.**

Psalm 119:33-34 TLB

FOR THE CLASS OF 2009

Faith never knows where it is being led, but it loves and knows the One who is leading.
—OSWALD CHAMBERS

We live by faith, not by sight.

2 Corinthians 5:7

The ideal man bears the accidents of life with dignity and grace, making the best of circumstances.
—ARISTOTLE

Give thanks in all circumstances, for this is God's will for you in Christ Jesus.

1 Thessalonians 5:18

FOR THE CLASS OF 2009

Leap, and the net will appear.
—John Burroughs

As for God, His way is perfect; the word of the LORD is proven; He is a shield to all who trust in Him.

2 Samuel 22:31 NKJV

FOR THE CLASS OF 2009

For it is in giving that we receive;
It is in pardoning that we are pardoned;
It is in dying that we are born to eternal life.
—St. Francis of Assisi

Even I, the Messiah, am not here to be served, but to help others, and to give my life as a ransom for many.

Mark 10:45 TLB

FOR THE CLASS OF 2009

Rare as is true love, true friendship is still rarer.
—JEAN DE LA FONTAINE

**I have called you friends, for
everything that I learned from my
Father I have made known to you.**

John 15:15

The greater part of our happiness or
misery depends on our disposition
and not our circumstances.
—MARTHA WASHINGTON

**I know how to live on almost nothing
or with everything. I have learned
the secret of contentment in every
situation.**

Philippians 4:12 TLB

FOR THE CLASS OF 2009

You can give without loving, but
you cannot love without giving.
—AMY CARMICHAEL

**It is more blessed to give than to
receive.**

Acts 20:35

FOR THE CLASS OF 2009

Honesty is the first chapter of the book of wisdom.
—THOMAS JEFFERSON

**You deserve honesty from the heart;
yes, utter sincerity and truthfulness.
Oh, give me this wisdom.**

Psalm 51:6 TLB

FOR THE CLASS OF 2009

Carve your name on hearts and not on marble.
—CHARLES H. SPURGEON

The only letter I need is you yourselves! … They can see that you are a letter from Christ, written by us …. Not one carved on stone, but in human hearts.

2 Corinthians 3:2–3 TLB

FOR THE CLASS OF 2009